ALSO BY BRENDA HILLMAN

POETRY

White Dress

Fortress

Death Tractates

Bright Existence

Loose Sugar

Cascadia

Pieces of Air in the Epic

CHAPBOOKS

Coffee, 3 A.M.

Autumn Sojourn

The Firecage

AS EDITOR

*The Grand Permission: New Writings
on Poetics and Motherhood*
[WITH PATRICIA DIENSTFREY]

The Poems of Emily Dickinson

*Writing the Silences: Selected Poems
of Richard O. Moore*
[WITH PAUL EBENKAMP]

PRACTICAL WATER

BRENDA HILLMAN

PRACTICAL WATER

WESLEYAN UNIVERSITY PRESS

MIDDLETOWN, CONNECTICUT

WESLEYAN POETRY

Published by Wesleyan University Press
Middletown, CT 06459

Copyright © 2009 by Brenda Hillman

Library of Congress Cataloging-in-Publication Data
Hillman, Brenda.
Practical water / Brenda Hillman.
p. cm.— (Wesleyan poetry)
ISBN 978-0-8195-6931-8 (cloth : alk. paper)
I. Title.
PS3558.I4526P73 2009
811'.54—dc22
2009012350

Design and composition by Quemadura
Printed on acid-free, recycled paper
in the United States of America

Wesleyan University Press is a member
of the Green Press Initiative. The paper
used in this book meets their minimum
requirement for recycled stock.

NATIONAL
ENDOWMENT
FOR THE ARTS
A great nation
deserves great art.

This project is supported in part by an award
from the National Endowment for the Arts.

This book is for my brothers, Brent & Brad Hillman

for Cal Bedient & Forrest Gander

for veterans of the current wars & CodePink

CONTENTS

ONE

TWO

THREE

FOUR

ONE

(OF INTERNATIONAL WATERS)

Water, whatever it communicates, remains always at a level.
DAVID HUME *Political Discourse of 1755*

As far as the eye sees, little garments of rain . . .
BARBARA GUEST "Constable's Method"

. . . the third commonness with light and air . . .
WALLACE STEVENS "A River of Rivers in Connecticut"

Though this bright world of all our joy is in the human brain . . .
WILLIAM BLAKE *The Book of Urizen*

We bury the sparrows of Europe
with found instruments,
their breasts light as an ounce of tea
where we had seen them off the path,
their twin speeds of shyness & notched wings
near the pawnbroker's house by the canal,
in average neighborhoods of the resisters,
or in markets of princely delphinium & flax,
flying from awnings at unmarked rates
to fetch crumbs from our table half-spinning
back to clefs of grillwork on external stairs
we would descend much later;

in rainy neighborhoods of the resisters
where streets were taken one by one,
where consciousness is a stair or path,
we mark their domains with notched sticks
of hickory or chestnut or ash
because our cities of princely pallor
should not have unmarked graves.
Lyric work, flight of arch, death bridge
to which patterned being is parallel:
they came as if from the margins
of a painting, their average hearts half-spinning
our little hourglass up on the screen.

PRACTICAL WATER

What does it mean to live a moral life

It is nearly impossible to think about this

We went down to the creek
The sides were filled
   with tiny watery activities

The mind was split & mended
Each perception divided into more

& there were in the hearts of the water molecules
   little branches perpendicular to thought

Had lobbied the Congress but it was dead
Had written to the Committee on Understanding
Had written to the middle
   middle of the middle
   class but it was drinking
Had voted in cafes with shoplifters &
   beekeepers stirring tea made of water
   hitched to the green arc

An ethics occurs at the edge
of what we know

The creek goes underground about here

The spirits offer us a world of origins
Owl takes its call from the drawer of the sky

Unusually warm global warming day out

A tiny droplet shines
    on a leaf & there your creek is found

It has borrowed something to
    link itself to others

We carry ourselves through the days in code
DNA like Raskolnikov's staircase neither
    good nor bad in itself

Lower frequencies *are* the mind
What happened to the creek
    is what happened
    to the sentence in the twentieth century
It got social underground

You should make yourself uncomfortable
If not you who

Thrush comes out from the cottony
    coyote bush glink-a-glink
        chunk drink
    trrrrrr
    turns a golden eyebrow to the ground

We run past the plant that smells like taco sauce

Recite words for water
    weeter wader weetar vatn
    watn voda
[insert all languages here]

Poor Rimbaud didn't know how to live
    but knew how to act
Red-legged frog in the pond sounds like him

Uncomfortable & say a spell:
blossom knit & heel affix
fiddle fern in the neck of the sun

It's hard to be water
    to fall from faucets with fangs
    to lie under trawlers as horizons
    but you must

Your species can't say it
You have to do spells & tag them

Uncomfortable & act like you mean it

Go to the world
Where is it
Go there

Sunlight tosses the small grasses its brain method. Once

    it gave us

    a dynamic hurt but we've gotten

             over it. Wobbly jay: the aspen is see-thru today,

       waiting for the Ice Age, & alphabets appear in

     every stem of it, tail shaking to a Y

    not far from ecstasy.

             The diverted creek sounds sad so maybe i better

take our dowsing stick out to the field, for our Y will

pull &

find buried water. With twig lines on our face & humming. With up &

       down for the world needs

    a water-finding stick for bringing wrecked water

sideways

beneath blue mist—   For water wants to be equal. Water wants

     to be equal & the world

        needs women with sticks & dusk husks, since they have

    taken the husks of damselflies when they straightened

    the creek, when the golf course needed its tight white

        globals (though the cowbird's yellow beanie eye

will survive the terrible pocked ball)—

Where there is a break in the fence near sweet horses we will skip

through

    & hold down our stick in a shiny chipping field, cabbage white

    butterflies in pairs, pennyroyal—   Diet Pepsi plastic on its side

& to the diverted creek & old creek bed

say Meet

      this dowsing wand Come in—

                    Mist rose this morning

as i crossed the field; heard the crooked cries cry creek to me,

      cried creek to me unable that the world wants

        water girls to work with mice, chipping off the blossom part of

    bitterbrush to save for later. Forced to mark

them out shy. Thanks for letting us know, hydrogen-times-two; leave

           the periodic

table & come to the dowsing stick, oxygen;

     come to the water table— we are taking this finding down to

        delphinium,

    angelica, mimulus, letting water go or we will go at night,

    among introduced grasses, under the moons called

Duir or Harvest,

Deer Paw the Earth & Gort, our stick

will dip down

in a y for

Yes

it's here. Aspen, don't quiver, there's root parties a plenty & we will be

    wicked with our wick in our turn—<   the stick will summon

meandering streams   for penstemon dandelion hair face,

    even the fungus beetle; those. Those qualities below. We miss

our mother.   Dear mother, daughter, pilot, poet, sister,

  student, teacher, waitress, worker, water girls & girlie men, don't do

their war; take y rods, angle rods, bobbers, pendulums & loops

for the stick is the witch with dew,

electrons & glaciers the stick does do;

for you miss your mother too & you can take your broken

    Y stick past the field they trapped energy in, poor stream,

        in their system there, to pull

                your water table up for water to be equal

like the warbler

        building nests against the imposter egg, will use that twig

    to mend the place where they have cut California in two.

    One at a time the simple

drops will come, though Agricola warned not to use the enchanted twig but

        you must come, it has

gotten serious!

So in binding oxygen to thin wild hydrogen & so in the earth you

    can bring energy from your

        stick signatures, earth's meridian roused from

  a source,

    we will squint our ears to the babble & make for them

    a wavelength over the old new field—

When we climbed the steps of the Capitol in the middle
　　　　of winter the middle of main, there were pale new
　　　　earthworms washed up on the steps, flat pink circles
　　　　around their necks as we passed the hollow in
　　　　the soldier's face where he sat in the park not thinking
　　　　of the law of If any man steal a minor son he shall be

put to death & so on. Shared light curled under the dome as we
　　　　walked. As we crossed. When we rose in the elevators,
　　　　we rode with platform managers & retail managers,
　　　　investors of mutual funds & stock options, with slim
　　　　portfolios that were feeling a little bullish, even slim women
　　　　were feeling a little bullish with their trim leather pouches

they took to the staff while the Dow was up & the up was down
　　　　past guards with chains that were effective. Through
　　　　double doors we walked with our stop-the-killing data
　　　　we brought through double central doors where If any
　　　　man put out the eye of another his eye shall be put out etc.
　　　　we went up dressed like sunrise, for the limits of color

are the limits of our girls. Officials waited like squid for us not
　　　　pretty of course like squid in the sea, propped up in
　　　　numbered offices when we took our motion in to them
　　　　but they flopped. Flopped floppety forward because of
　　　　having no spines. Floppety forward they couldn't sit up.
　　　　Washington knows best, said Room 2141, Probably not

but Hmm said Mr. Speaker himself. Maybe Yes but No, said Ed
in 2148. Why try, said Jenny O. Here is some cake!
It was written on the wall past the chief-of-staff's head
that If any man harm the captain injure the captain
or take away from the captain a gift presented to him
by the king he shall be put to death Raised Seal

Not Required. Thanks for dropping by! said the Canciamilla-
squid as we read the writing past his plutocrat head, in
endless vengeance decimals of pi, two eyes for an eye,
he said, Bye, ladies, goodbye! As we carried our vitamin
shadows out. As we shook their flaccid tentacles off.
As we slipped. When we slipped down the steps

in the middle of rain, the earthworms adjusted the alphabet so
the next thing may not be the next thing, they wrote.
They spelled in calligrammes & codes. When they
brought back Ishtar's cuneiform. For the love of myrtle,
cedar & rose that came from dust. The vine sisters
twisted in stone as they turned in earth to speak to us.

RHOPALIC AUBADE

And
a black-
bird follows
you from city
to city, changing
names as it flies (osle,
merula); it sheds its first
music at daybreak (Amsel) as
it drops letters that will float in a
river of your father (lon dubh, lon dobh)
or into the slight raindrops of your mother
(melro, merle noir), onto a forest or desert floor
(merlo, karatavuk, κότσυφας) where the ochre
worm feeds quietly in starlight. With a ring around its
famous eye (kostrast), restless and a little shy between trills
at night (musträsas, zozo), it flies to places where gods are called
Disposers and yet are commensurate with life. So when another
name springs open in your heart (komunsae, 검은새, mirlo, кос, kos)
—or in the aqua crucible of dawn—syllable and bird (merel, svarttrost)
long for each other in the description, dragging lovers to light (mustarastas,
solsort), dragging meanings as dense and particular as food or as pieces of songs,
as existence that hopes for itself (juodasis stazdas, черный дрозд, chernyi drozd, Al-
Ta'er, الشحرور, A-Sho'hroor, רורתש, Sha-ch-rur) as spaces in songs after morning—

INTERNATIONAL DATELINE

A row of hyphens exists in the sea

You squint to find it x miles down

You saw it in the magazine
& eyeless fish that swim under it

You left one perfect day for your friends

What will they do with a perfectly left day
watching clouds on Yellow Mountain

touched by night in the Hall of Speaking

A row of red hyphens exists in the sea in scales
of fish in dropped-back hours

You the seer of your life
your friends the seers of theirs

touched by sunrise on one side only
before a moon touches you on the other

in blue or local blue eternal time

They keep you with you   you keep them with them

You keep them with you
They keep you with them

AN ESSAY

A friend asks, "What was at stake for you in the Eighties?" She's trying to figure out Bay Area Poetry. There was Reagan's New Morning for America. Garfield dolls stuck to the backs of windshields with suction cups. At the beginning of the Eighties I was married & at the end i was not. The Civil Rights Movement became kind of quiet. Feminism became kind of quiet. An editor told a woman he couldn't read her poems because it said she was a *mother* in her bio. Many thought about word materials. Environmentalism got kind of quiet. The earth spirits were not quiet. Buildup of arms. Iran-Contra. Savings & Loan scandal. Tax cuts gave way to library closings. The *Challenger* went down with the first woman astronaut aboard. People read letters to her on TV. Mini-golf places with purple castles opened on Highway 80 in the Eighties. Chernobyl exploded & the media announced it as a setback for nuclear energy. People ate out more because of tax cuts. i fell in love with a poet. Earth dropped its dark clock. A few wrote outside the margins. Mergers & Acquisitions. The Bay continued to shrink. Many got child-support checks. Many came out. Deconstruction found the moving circle. A few read Lacan. Guns 'n Roses Sweet Child o' Mine. Our daughter drew pictures of trucks with colored fur. She had 24 ear infections in one year so why were you not supposed to write *mother* in your bio. Many wrote the lyric with word materials. The Soviet Union began to free prisoners. America freed fewer prisoners. Superconductivity. Gorbachev became president instead of something else. One son went to college. We cried. There was no e-mail. Art pierced the image. Blue-rimmed clouds hurried past outside & in. Some wrote about childhood; some wrote about states of mind; some wrote word materials instead of about. Symbolist poetry, by then 120 years old, pushed the dream nature of the world. Hypnotherapy. i began the trance method. In the Eighties, Mt. Tam stayed the same. Mt. Diablo stayed almost the same. Many species died & would not return. At stake. One son started a punk band; he had a one-foot-high purple Mohawk. i listened to the tape with another mother trying to make out the words. Oliver North held up his right hand. Reagan turned off his hearing aid. Sentences fell apart but they had always been a part. Yeltsin. Walesa. Wall comes down. Romania. El Salvador. Noriega. Some elderly folk lived on dog-food when their pensions collapsed. People worried about children, lovers, ex-husbands, jobs. Consciousness stayed alive. Interest rates leapt through the vault of the sky. We cried & cried. We made food & quit smoking. We learned the names of wildflowers & forgot them & relearned them. This was only the beginning. There's so much more to be said in answer to your question.

(i looked up from my reading;
the one who is
always visiting
stood on the rug
in one of her Europe moments;

i asked her whether
i should be writing
when i'm not writing or
not writing when
i'm not writing—)

PHONE BOOTH

There should be more nouns
For objects put to sleep
Against their will
The "booth" for instance
With coiled hidden wires
Lidded chrome drawers
Tipping up like lizards' eyes
We looked out into rhymed rain
We heard varying vowels
Rimbaud's vowels with colors
Orange or blue beeps
Types of ancient punctuation
The interpunct between words
A call became twenty-five cents
Times in a marriage we went there
To complain or flirt
Two more decades & we wised up
Got used to the shadow
The phone booth as reliquary
An arm could rest
On the triangular shelf
A briefcase between the feet
A pen poked into acoustic holes
While we gathered actions/wits
For magic & pain
The destiny twins
Folks scratched pale glyphs
Onto the glass door while talking

One day we started to race past
& others started racing
Holding phones to their ears
Holding a personal string
To their lips
If there are overages
There might be nouns for
The clotting of numbers in the sky
So thick the stars can't shine through
A word for backing away
From those who shout to their strings
In the airport while eating
We loved the half booths
Could cup one hand on the mouthpiece
Lean two-thirds out to talk to a friend
Sitting in the lobby
The universe grows
We are dizzy as mercury
We are solitudes aided by awe
Let us mourn secrets told to
Fake wood & the trapezoidal seat
Perfume in the mouthpiece
Like a little Grecian sash
Why did we live so fast
The booth hid our ankles
We twisted the rigid cord
As we spoke
It made a kind of whorl

TIERGARTEN SCENES

Berlin 2002

HERCULES BRIDGE

Perhaps it's average to want not to have failed
          an experience. I have sensed this in cities

just as between rungs of a bridge there are sunbeam
          sway curls, as if between emotions
          there were livelier half-states

where it could be Wednesday afternoon & something would sail:

a humming syllable enters a coil, a whorl of blue pollen
          over a lake, a companionable loneliness, the hair

          of the maenads who could destroy you.

I was interested in the place where pain & pleasure
          were made worse & better by life among others.

"DECISIVE BENCHES" (WALTER BENJAMIN)

Linked in swirling sun with

sugar ovals from

their breasts, in outskirts of a city

park, your mourning

·

for syntax   finds   momentary
rest   where the Other   throbbed—

NEW LAKE

Minnows mix artless but best domains
                    with minuet fear

here where the park is without angles, the swans
                    are mean, & hug the lake.

We join the style of Sunday strolling as if 1932
                    were quiet   in warm shade; people pass
                    with special sighs

& the sense we fall into   (the half-feeling

as if by obsession with historical distance, as if the terrible
                    could be   pre-avoided—)

is that to perceive, beyond perception   frees the pattern—

minnows with plusses or fire signs on their tails—

LICHTENSTEIN BRIDGE

At the country resistance canal, near where Rosa was thrown in,

lovers lean over . . . their sexual intensity, their point of view—
                    der Gesichtspunct— ;

every moment so intimate, the water cannot relate.

You read history on the bench. Just beyond
                        your book: letters float upstream.

Unable to prevent a "next" by reading, stalled in a sequence—
                        as if in terror or mysticism—you call

on the meaningful & numbered past.

AUTUMN FUGUE

A book was sometimes held in your hand
when the Committee on Understanding met
as you waited for them to call you in
& the man who mowed the graveyard
waved with a circular wave
in the manner of cousins under the elm
where it seemed sweet spices
had been cast down near accordion streets
so once the small democracies
had begun, time could make an exception
for owls with the faces of seeds
that looked just like themselves only open;

it is late & sweet with a late
democratic sweetness when seeds
had been cast down in the manner of
spices, where once the small committees
had begun, time played accordion
with its foot in the door, & you felt
at ease in a circular way
so even had the parties called your name
you would not have been wrong;
the elms had made an exception
& a book was sometimes found in your hand
that looked just like itself, only open—

SHADOWS IN SNOW

When shadows are unhinged from bodies,
        they make chords with clouds
        impossible to hear.

In the end, there will be nothing wrong.
Tonight red ring surrounds the moon
like a hurt boy
following a married woman;

you hurry along, tired of your travels,

& the dense beauty from whose demands
        you never recover
stays beside you
as the orchid keeps the black stripe
of its personal winter—

LANDING IN FOG

... the sea anemone dreamed of something ... (OPPEN)

i hated hated hated hated hated leaving my mother
yet i know the great heart of the world is whole particulars like % signs

i cry most of the way to California not just for my mother but for Bonhoeffer
where he writes *Stellvertretung* ("vicarious representative action") while
in prison for plotting to kill Hitler then hold the *Ethics* on my lap & stop crying
      because it's all so odd

The pilot's voice enters the cabin in charged diagonals, enters the body
      of the woman who struggles to open her peanuts, first the serrated top
      then the uniquely inadequate notch at the side

On the wing the lumpy x's in big screws holding the plane together

There's a trustworthy mist over Santa Monica

A dainty mist the first bacteria must have loved when they finished
      eating volcanoes

Comforting to think of the place where water meets fire
Creatures with impossibly-colored gelatinous bodies

Perhaps Rimbaud is there, as is Gandhi

Wondering about the expression *as a crow flies*

Looks from here like the crow flies between lavender moon rinds & Saturn
      or between Regulus & a bunch of galaxies with names like Beehive

PACIFIC OCEAN

{a p'ansori}

To feel emotion   underneath emotion   (a fertile dread
had mixed   with ecstasy,   not delight   such as delight

in nature   but of nature—   a brew,   a brink—;)

i went   to the ocean,   my hydrogen host,   was greeted in   the negation
of the moment   finding itself;   put my hand   to the surface & felt

the surface   of emotion: a calm inside   the prize,   the gold halves

beyond   the terms of argument   & terrifying   acts of intent.   When

first people sailed   in basket boats to never the place   envisioning
an ideal,   did the pelican   pass them   as here it passes—   its fine

head of z's?   Russian forts, frigates,   a bit of fathom—   Drake strides
onto land,   his sailors' lives   handcuffed   to expectation

(a borderous   dream   is a dream—)

Everything   i cried out   & you embraced me: First threads   of life,
paradise parasite—   & have you heard   in juvenile gull-squeals (dent in

its beak)   the deaf 'we are'   braiding itself?   Dulse, red algae,   brown kelp

sizes us back . . . i cast myself   before   the mind's trough—skin tent . . .

& the sun 'rose' a billion   days in a saint's   circle of spikes . . .

Was aware of your   west,   volcanic aperture   where flounder   has no timing
was aware of your   south;   & suppose   a flock   of beautiful ones   wanted

neither to leave nor long—or . . . not wanted, exactly; between you
& it: amorous blood—   (or so Agrippa writes of water's magic)—

The "will"   before life's great cry — fear plus splendor, fame of joy,
internal skill to pause . . .   Carbon landed in no atmosphere;   plastic

(in the first sense)   pre-eucaryote lineage—a trellis before
membranes (particular membranes . . . thicknesses—)

the sun rose a billion days   like the remorse of a bachelor.

Sea foam   condensed from early skins. i had a   temporary joy—
We stand   as a child in brenda's body   (thought forms—theosophy)

It is a long time   before they'll ruin you dumping phosphates

dumping degrees of   plastic of   (of   of   of)   an I stands

kicking the foam,   coughing; there are   surnames   of stars   in the salt . . .

When they stood here (or rather, environments. Environments
stood here) bacteria assembled before skins.   Rods, twitching stick-

shapes,   frenzied plates   or disks,   dismantling   minerals to hoard
fevers, in tenses—no duplicates at first sheen.   Steam stolen from

volcanoes . . . Specific families are inside cabins, laughing, playing

flat games, laughing,   waves lapping to this:

> *Great mother protect my mother*
> *Great ocean protect my father*
> *Great future protect the brothers*
> *& i saw a ring of stars in the water*

Copepods, jellyfishes allow   through tunnels of bodies
our laughter— you are not "endangered" yet . . . One day   i will be

the word "fumerole"— pharaoh yellow of same sun, the sex of touch—
(probably.   Probably touched.)   Red tide,   brown tide, young

young ocean.   Volcanoes called black smokers. Deep hills' blind
forms breathed into   convolute curls of the mollusk (to which Benjamin

compared   a living room in Paris)—my   heart closed   each time i felt
& when it opened   we were science. Don't say lost.   Ocean, we

had been your   griot. Could you hear   backward? Pull
of the window   shade, the waxen eye . . .

Emotions came   so late to earth;   hope passing through   the what . . .

Ocean has consonants, vowels & continents; it is a while   before
they'll ruin you . . . Life was found,   as is   commonly thought. The mat

of pre-cells puffed   & puffed. Puff-puff. Ha.

& the sun "rose" a million days, like a proud   nephew—

> *Great mother protect the other*
> *Great ocean protect the otter*
> *Great godwit protect the godwit*
> *& i saw a ring of stars in the water.*

Splendor, panic in awe, fear of envy, ragged   shame—propitiatory
dawns make emotions matter. Starfishes evolve: bath-mat   bumps

on them,   nucleic acids looking so Cyrillic, Urdu,   Hangeul—
a cormorant stands by, in its 40s   movie detective trench-coat. Balm

to talk to you, ocean ... Apophatic.   An ocean has   no   summary in tears.

Initiating curls of s-light change themselves   to pre-again, blue-green
algae   finds   carbon   for breath ...   Names touch & leave: benthos,

nekton,   neuston, plankton— "eco-poetry"   families   of anemones
waiting   for visitors,   pink nubbly prickles   defined

to wheel the gritty mollusks   in— (poets, save the names)

& the sun "rose"— Ahem,   like a civil servant ...

You came so late to earth before life's great cry— Summer
in the spine,   types of tides (Neap tide, violet &   rare ...)

Beige & other mists fall   into footprints;   a thousand skinny

flies squint in my ear; it is a while   before they'll ruin you—

Removed my hat, my shoes. China's. Removed   China's shoes.
Socks. Removed   China's socks. Shirt from the Philippines,

hair thing from Korea; rings.   Europe's rings. Took off my
rings & walked   in—not to die ... Baptists like to merge,

shamans like to   fly. Through years,   the bodies— near footprints,
moats, with brothers,   friends   when i am not them;

otters' skins near Pt. Lobos— (almost wrote logos) in furry hecate
moonlight & further south   where you take tiny raindrops to

Santa Monica's   pier-legs coarse clingy beards holding mussels on—
Why were we 'life' &   not nothing, she sang—   clans & tribes

& the sun rises like   a high school reunion, wise because past ...

Methane to carbon.   Membranes assembled without air; shreds
of light snagged   cynobacteria, plates,   circlets & disks,   nibblers

of sulfur, clans & chimes.   We will name them   siphonophore, for
whom "the crowd   is no veil,"   will name them   miracle, twin x's,

plover,   shark with   pursed vat-mouth, will call them   beer-can-
off-Stinson,   circumference,   sargassum weed,   radial gleam off

the Farallones . . . why   were we this   & not nothing, she sang,

she might have sung . . . i sang but i don't do beyond;
i do beside. Beside the ~~~~ . . . & so on—

The tide is low &   safe;   water,   twin energy, heard shell shard
scales,   plank & plankton   in minnows through   plastic six-pack

holder looks like   θθθ   except for what happened is : it was endless—

The body turns   35, 8, 53, 81, 42—it graduates to timeless & drinks
violins . . . Beach flies around brown   kelp, brown of beak & burin,

sandpiper wild in sanderlings' syllable colony, shadows

like wine in a cave in Montara after the hurt joy . . . It is while
they'll try to   ruin you . . . Emotions learn to fold themselves

as does   ∞infinity∞ : fin in it,   then in in   that, i in in,
energy & pure   annihilation merge in words, it said once; it said that . . .

(see spice routes,   http://asiapacificuniverse.com/pkm/spiceroutes.htm)

what about specific 'maritime routes'? (i love the word "maritime")—

First bacteria, rods   in their backs, disk-stems . . . & then evolved
the forked gull- feet, then   love,   its beulah dream of awe . . .

Century, come here   a minute & let's sing for the ocean:

> *Virginia, don't drown.*
> *Gertrude, Mina, Hilda,*
> *Marianne. Anna, Marina,*
> *Elizabeth, Lorine, Muriel,*
> *Gwendolyn, Cecília, Sylvia*
> *don't drown. Denise. Barbara—*

A verbed set of dolphins scallop on by toward San Diego. (Hi
Rae.) A cloud goes by, puff-,   parallel to economics. Puff-puff.

Microcontinents   deeper than glades. Pelagic. Love   appears as
measure,   a wreath of instances—

> *Great ocean protect the husband*
> *Great future protect the daughter*
> *Specific ocean protect the student*
> *& i saw a ring of stars in the water*

The tide was low &   safe. Lots of low   laughing to draw emotion   in—

Ocean, you   exist as signs. Nature, you exist as   ocean. Everything,
you've become quite advanced   (for an everything)— Horizon strings,

nodes . . . Quarry jewels.   Marine   squall squalling on up— golden colony
clumps.   It is summer days   in California   with jellyfish,   & in

the   mid-Pacific rift   where fish are blind,   the giant squid has writing in its eye, the   song has   glass sides like a diatom—

& near   the lighthouse   orange lichen steps,   pet apocalypse stars
fall down . . . did did did did too,   we saw them—

Countries, drop your   countries.
Paraclete gull drop   signs in a ring. Poets, drop nothing;

you are asked   to do the blind   extraordinary thing—

the dream seminars go   on & on   beside which   you are

the shaking   figment — coiled life. Up & under & in—

TWO

(OF COMMUNAL AUTHORITY)

*To be political, to live in a polis, meant that everything was decided
through words and persuasion and not through force and violence.*

HANNAH ARENDT *The Human Condition*

Know your rights   all three of them.

THE CLASH "Know Your Rights"

Do you remember the corpse in the basement?
What are we doing at the turn of our years,
Writers and readers of the liberal weeklies?

KENNETH REXROTH "August 22, 1939"

In the event of a water landing,
the slide may be used as a raft.

FLIGHT ATTENDANT ON UNITED AIRLINES

FLIGHT 914 TO WASHINGTON DULLES

Reportorial poetics can be used to record detail with immediacy while one is doing an action & thinking about something else.

 Experience crosses over with that which is outside experience; the unknown receives this information as an aquifer receives replenishing rain. Meditative states can be used to cross material boundaries, to allow you to be in several places at once, such as Congress & ancient Babylon.

I recorded notes in Washington while attending hearings & participating in actions to make the record collective & personal. Working with trance while sitting in Congressional hearings i recorded details into a notebook.

If bees can detect ultraviolet rays, there are surely more possibilities in language & government. The possible is boundless.

Whether or not you have strength to resist official versions that are devastating the earth & its creatures, you could in any case send back reports. If political parties will not provide solutions, the good can occur when people gather in small groups to work for justice in each community using imagination without force.

People could leave their computers at least briefly to engage with others in public spaces. It is then the potential of each word comes forward.

If you have no time or strength, act without time or strength because they may follow. In the meantime you could imagine that you have them.

From my position as a woman
        i could see
                the back of the General's head, the prickly
intimate hairs behind his ears,
                the visible rimless justice raining down
from the eagle on the national seal,
        the eagle's claw-held pack of arrows
            & its friends. A fly was making its for-sure-maybe-
algebra cloud in the Senate chamber; it fell to us
                to see how Senators
re-shuffled papers, the pity of
        the staples, to sense when someone coughed after
                    the about-to-be-czar General said *I don't foresee a long
role for our troops,* there was a rose vibration in the rug.
        From its position on the table the fly
could then foresee
                the soon-to-be-smashed goddess as in
    Babylon. More perception had to be, began to be.
        Filaments rose from the carpet as the General spoke,
the Senators were stuck. What
                were they thinking sitting there
        as dutiful as lunch patrols
in junior high. From my position as the fly

i could foresee as letters issued
from their mouths like *General I'd be interested*
　　to know, some of the letters regretted that.
　　　　　　　　　　　　Fibers in the carpet
　　　　　crouched. From
the floor arose the sense
　　　　　　　　the goddess Ishtar had come down
　　to bring her astral light with a day-wrinkled plan. From my position
　　　　　as a thought i thought she might. She might
　　　come in to rain her tears
on Senator Bayh & Senator Clinton, on Senator Warner
　　　　　　　　　　in his papa tie & Senator Levin, on Senator Reed &
Senator Hill—rain tears into their water glasses, Ishtar
　　　from Babylon they had not met
　　　　before they smashed her country now or never.
　　　　　　　　　　Then someone—Clinton i think it was
but it might have been Bayh—asked whether this confirmation *will*
　　　　　　　　give breathing space for the new
　　　General to unoccupy (*how do the dead breathe, Senator,* from my position
　　　　　　　　as a fly) & i forget who asked what isn't even
　　　in the same syntax of this
language i'm trying to make no progress in, asked
　　　　　how the army would unoccupy, by north or south?
A voice beside my insect ear
　　　　　said, these Senators all have their lives:
　　　　　kids with stuff to do, folks with cancer, some
　　　　　　　　secret shame in a quotidian—
the thing in front always producing

panic,—just like yours, the voice went, just like your life.
i tried to think if this was true but was too weak from
         flying above this notebook to pity them. From my
              position as a molecule i could foresee
twelve Senate water glasses, each bubble had an azure
         rim, the ovals on
the Senators' heads were just like them, the breath they used
when saying °° *A* °° for *American interests* made the *A* stand still,
              it had a sunset clause.
    They tried to say °°° *Safety* °°° but the *S* withdrew,
the *S* went underground. Would not
be redeployed. Refused to spell. Till all the letters stopped
         in astral light, in dark love for their human ones—

We tune
We tune we ginseng
We client rubbing against us heel as high
They serpentine
We padlock the ten mists
We eat military
We eat the curly kale
We eat the curly kitchen heel as high
She Shasta
She triangle train-track Shasta
She Ishtar the set of roses be as high
She waitress
She finger to help
We cubicle silicon
They purification chanting hand as high
She melting
She Milton a thousand pages
We lawyer the miners' lettuce
They xerox the busted motive
She shoot some voicelet movie
They Sacramento pinko
They anger turning yellow
You comrade turning yellow
She cancer the ten mists hand as high
You antiwar pneumonia
We void the drowsy element
She Ishtar the element until she die
She puppet she paint the puppet puppet
They keep the dragon bookstore
They sip the twenty decaf
Twenty rusty roses occupy
She dusky-footed wood rat

She western flycatcher teacher Pwee-pwee
She kisst Apollo honey
We kiss Apollo honey i kiss Apollo honey till we die
i driplet
O driplet driplet
O braised fog elderberry no slant slump
She best equestrian surfer
She persona knowna
She park the tilden children
She oak slug-shrinker diviner be as high
We aspen flutter against us
We deaf light rubbing against us
They freeway rubbing against us
She traintrack history alone
She puff puff history home
She cloud cloud cloud cloud passing through our hipbone

DRAGONSKIN

There's a useful panic like the secret script
sent between women in villages. Right now
it's a series of marks i'm making   ··· :::: ::: ::
            during a subcommittee hearing
on body armor while they ask the salesman
        from a weapons plant in Virginia
about a fabric called Dragonskin
            (i write this in my notebook as *DRAGONSKIN*
slash slash shash slash—[fairly art-deco]—"used
            to make body shields more comfortable in the desert ····")
The Congress folks are tired & beige, the hearing table like 2/3
        of a horseshoe from a corral without horses

& each time someone says *Dragonskin* i feel the panic
        or subpanic as from school when certain
    steady voices had set in & we made light natural dots
            in a string :::: ····· ··· or a set of *therefores* (:: :: :)
        which, when i'm placing parentheses now,
            Microsoft keeps changing to a happy face— (:: ☺
The calm in adult talk sets this going if
        there are no modulating tones around it—;
my heart makes tiny confidential dots ··· :: ·· :: ··

& i've read that women in remote villages in China
            invented script men couldn't read ·· · :::: ···
            breathprints of a neutrino entering
                earth through a rain cloud ···· sending whispers
    with it . . . When the Congressman asks Has Dragonskin
been shown in tests to be more lightweight than the material
being presently used in armor & if so Is it less
            scratchy, the salesman states Yes & Congressman
asks Side-by-side tests? & the salesman states Dragonskin

was tested by NBC [not for NBC, by NBC]
& the Congressman asks You're sure it's superior & the salesman
        replies I didn't say superior I believe
        I said it was better & the Congressman breathes out God
        bless the Marines—

i've always thought dragons have soft skin but not as tender
        as a human nipple; it could resemble
    the reddish skin of the endangered newt
that makes its way with nervous depth in the drizzle sensing
        it's alone on earth & when we see it ···:::::¨
    we're not supposed to grab it . . .
                    The Congressmen love fingering the Dragonskin;
they love its hidden speckles. Someone
        notes its weight is 1 or 19—
        i'm not sure 19 whats. This is no declensionist narrative;
        the order of things is unclear in this next part.
Calm & shadowy (:::: ::: :: ··· i'm writing you
    in secret) Empire, destruction, imagination & wilderness—

There, in the same
spot as the annihilation
of the world, love
of existence stood. We
walked along. In boulevard
windows: plates, hatlike napkins
set for an imaginary
meal. Each act of
revenge has love as
a twin, but could
art convey this without
violence? In this parabola,
i recalled the little
dragon in the painting,
that high, curly arch
of its tail like
a syntax being inaugurated.
Polka-dots on emerald wings.
The knight stabbed it;
maybe the vertical princess
prayed for it to live.
This was the end
of time. Dread had
not returned to listen.

Shelley wants you to visit Congress when he writes
    a violet in the crucible & when he notes
        imagination is enlarged by a sympathy
that you may intuit environments
as endangered creatures do when 7 million pounds
    of nitrogen flow into the Chesapeake—;
as you push open the cherry wood door
    & the intern looks up from her
map of wheels beside the philodendron with streaked
anemic arrows & a jar
        of pens from pharmaceutical firms,
 Shelley knows you are endangered
    as the eyeless shrimp *Stygobromus hayi* living
        among rocks upstream in Virginia feeding on dying
    leaves is, or the Congressman you came to visit
    is endangered, feeding
in the Rayburn cafeteria with the lobbyist from Bechtel, having left his
aide endangered in a faux-maple carrel
    to work on the war funding bill
        where seedlings of the law have finished sprouting.
    You look at things to make them speak.
    You have threadlike legs found only in your species.
The cogs are selling credits to the dams
    for phosphorous to go into the sea.
When Shelley says ‹ the poet is the legislator › he means as
    the duskytail darter from Tennessee legislates or
the Indiàna bat, *myotis sodalist*, the dwarf wedgemussel
        half buried in Maryland with your bivalve
        in silt of your wetland habitat, as you, the vanishing
northeastern bulrush from Massachusetts
    legislate by shrinking; he doesn't mean you will live,
he means you could live on listen. As the sturgeon

in a million pounds of phosphorous or
the snowy plover from Cascadia might.
The aide is living on listen too,
he takes your words, there's a little you
in his left eye which tries to focus on your nervous
speech, a stubby tassel
swinging on his shoe; he's got a friend in the Marines
who likes it over there instead of working
in the tire shop after high school. The punctuation
falling from your eyes its eyes their eyes his eyes
is merging with uh·· uh·· uh·· uh·· uh·· uh·· as he explains
the Pentagon budget uh·· uh·· uh·· uh·· his sentences forming
a five-star alkaline: *We cannot leave them*
there without weapons uh-uh-uh-uhuhuh.
He cannot see the stars camped in your heart,
the bunchy bunched-up stars, though he also
has stars in his heart & his friend the Marine has stars.
When Shelley notes ‹ the poet is meant to cheer › he means
your name is on the list right here, he means
if you don't survive this way there are others,
he means send the report with your body—

A brenda is missing—where is she?
Summon the seeds & weeds, the desert whooshes. Phone the finch
with the crowded beak;   a little pretenda
        is learning to read
in the afternoon near the cactus caves. Near oleander & pulpy
caves with the click-click of the wren & the *shkrrrr* of the thrasher,
        a skinny pretenda is learning
to read till the missing brenda
        is found. Drip of syllables like olives near the saguaro.
Nancy Drew will find the secret in raincoats & wednesdays
        & sticks. Nancy whose spine is yellow
        or blue will find the brenda in 1962,
Nancy   who has no mother,
        who takes suggestions from her father & ignores them.

Gleam goes the wren ignoring the thorn. They cannot tell the difference.
Click of the smart dog's nails on linoleum.
                        Nancy bends over the clues,
of brenda's locket & dress. Word by word
        between syllables a clue. Where has the summer gone, the autumn—
are they missing too? Maybe Nancy
        will parse the secret & read the book report on Nancy Drew:
"neat pretty sly cute." Syllable by syllable
        & still no brenda!   Nancy
puts her hand to her forehead; is the missing
girl in the iron bird? is the clue to the girl in the locket?

The sniper on the roof of the White House could be a boy hunting lizards
  in the suburbs, someone whose mother is dutiful & unique, whose
  father taught him to tripod his legs when he aims at a woman
  whose son is in Kirkuk, at the protesting Buddhist in the knit vest

& at the character known as I before she blends in with the woman next
  to us whose son's coffin was unloaded from the hold of the c-17 Globe-
  master by Boeing after they unloaded the rations & dogs;

through the crosshairs of his scope he can see the poet who thinks she
  knows more than he does but they both learned precision in their
  work for the unseen;

the President, having lunch below, takes a sip of juice; he is warm in the middle
  like a boiled egg & his body has outwitted the search;

all of them are right according to themselves & they will never meet. An anar-
  chist called the Future is right as it lowers itself into them in a series
  of nouns: cancer, teaching, Buddhism, Starbucks, reggae, time, the
  poem, Crawford, Practical Water, Kirkuk, time, cancer, the search;

it lowers itself into you reading this, your hope is the next breath, you do your
  best, your hope is breath;

the Future does not like to rest as art likes to, in objects; it tosses particulars
  that wash over us like the great sea,

it knows there is only everything as it invents the pointillist method in painting
  in the nineteenth century, invents the boy & his targets in the
  twentieth, invents this type of writing under the guise of speech in a
  dream like the dream the eighteenth century had of functional beauty
  where the boy points his neighborhood gun at you in a city made up
  of of of little little dot-dot-dots of color

Triangular shadows
arrive on your wall
with music from the street
behind them . . . Like you
they are from autumn between
those spirits, not from any thing.

They need you to see them
finding width & depth from
noon or moon, these figures,
eking thought around vines
in a time of violence
leaking fact into eternity.

You are given permission
to be strange in these outlines
from the vat
of what you feel. They walk
the wall, rinsed &
rosy, not from any thing.

You make energy matter &
individual with lines
between parts of experience.
Conductivity, the gray
fur of feeling
wild from anything—

A man says he doesn't understand my poetry

Frankly i'm not surprised

I learned to write in a hot desert during the cold war
We did air raid drills in a schoolyard full of thick-skinned
    ornamental oranges

We saw dioramas of a fallout shelter where a mother wearing a light
    print housedress served TV dinners on aluminum trays to children
    wearing saddle shoes

The man says poetry should be simple enough
    for school girls to understand

But sir, school girls understand everything

Nancy Drew was in love with the obstacle not the clue

My nearsighted eyes had adjusted to reading & by 1962
    letters had developed fuzzy antennas like tarantulas or modernism

The psyche rises like mist from things, writes Heraclitus

Sir, when i think of poetry keeping you alive i know
    you were entered by incomprehensible light
    in the hour of lemon & water

& the great wound of the world has slipped a code
    into your shoe

A poem doesn't fail when you set your one good wing on the ground

It is the wing
It doesn't abandon you

It would be lovely to ask water to investigate

        domestic spying so i put myself in a trance

                right here in Congress holding a bottle of H_2O

from California so when the Principal Deputy Assistant

        Attorney General reads *probable cause to believe*

                the water shakes its curly geyser brain &

when he says *need to close the gaps* it shakes times 3 until its letters

        break & splash to the floor of the Rayburn Building

                OHH-OHH-OHH-OHH-OHH

        OHH-OHH during the report about reading

                your e-mail. Maybe it's not your e-mail.

From the 2nd row it's possible to see white ridges in his

                thumbnails while he holds *surveillance has to be*

reasonable as the prong-prong molecules <<<< of water

                trickle through the carpet to find

        the vault where the Electronic $urveillance

Modernization Act, the Terrorist $urveillance Act, the National

$ecurity $urveillance Act & the Foreign

        Intelligence $urveillance Improvement &

                Enhancement Act are stashed to hide them

        from the mobs of 1772. There's a secret

in every act down there. i hear some water interview the ants

        who make the basic laws of the land & while

the Deputy reads *ferret out terrorists* the water interviews

        a ferret under Capitol Mall that can't quite

streamline operations in the ruddy soil. Perspective is gained;

      the trance method seems to be working well.

i can see half a heart in each Congressman;

      i can see the Deputy has a shaving cut &

a sunbeam shining through the skin of his left ear,

        it's feeling rather prone, the light, its pink

     the color of winter robins' legs that

makes me want not to hate him. It's the tendency

      of light to change itself. He probably has two

    kids & lives in Fairfax near where Whitman's

mockingbird spends winters; he was sprinkled with birth,

     his death floats near the secrets he can't read.

There's a clue in every word down there. When he says

    has to be reasonable the droplets

       splash their skinny necks & swelling Buddha

bellies & break to make CAPITOL HILL spell I TOLL

      or TOP AL ILL. You at home, what do you feel.

   You can vote by calling 1-900-it's-either-too-fucking-

     late-or-too-early. There's

a secret in every century that likes it

    if you shout. There is time for our little secret.

There is space for the secret spilling out.

IN THE TRANCE

A pretty anarchist said to me
It's not that a great love happens
What happened became your great love

Her echo had an ancient glow & so
proved buoyant for my little craft

I left the world & felt a world

The bee loading its gloves with powder
The albatross wanting one thing from the sea

Nothing can wreck our boat said she

& when the water felt the glacier
The future held a present tense
The present held a future without cease

I'm sick of irony

Everything feels everything

Everything returns to earth

There are no spaces between us

If you walk past the U.S. Securities & Exchange Commission
    numbers speak in color
    by the order of the dream

Chartreuse 4s talk to blue 8s
    9s speak yellow
    There is fever in the badges of the guards

Inside the Federal Reserve
    humans twirl the national debt
    on its orange 3s
    & the gray 11s are spinning too

Humans take a pile of blue 8s from a teacher in Des Moines
    & spin them to day-traders in Cancun

They take brown 5s from a waitress in Detroit
    & give them to gamers in L.A.

If it is warm you can send yourself out
    as a 7 because 7s can fly

They fly over buy-out specialists
    lobbyists drinking lattes
    with classic sweetener nearby

If you go to the Capitol
    you can send reports to the provinces
    of astounding sights you saw there

Numbers plot as you walk to Congress
    like Italian anarchists from Petaluma
    in 1948

Rooftop trees make a pirate flapping
    as you walk from Union Station
There is fever in the badges of the guards

I'm sick of irony
Everything feels everything
Feels itself as nearly lived
    even colorless floating dollars
    that have done violence &
    have lain down to absorb the blood
    & fluttered home to die

Numbers feel as they are spent
    2s tinged with cinnamon
    migrate over commodity policies

Your great reliable love will never be used up

You are very tired i know

You shouldn't have to travel

But in your wisdom
    you can send yourself out
    as a shaman pushes himself
    from the mouth of a lily
    to fly over the Pentagon clutching

a chrome 10 or a vermillion 6
to enter the world with feeling

People on their lunch breaks
    are reading nearly weightless
    novels on benches in the park
    making 9 to 5s with their legs
    eating take-out
    feeding bits of tuna wrap to
    Capitol Hill squirrels

A poem changes nothing

This isn't a political poem
There are no results in poetry

A shaking doubt has instructed you
    to address the long wars
    with short cries

Not to live against earth
You who have so little time

You to whom others have written

You a citizen of matter & beyond

THREE

(OF THE MONTHS WHEN YOU WORK

& THE MONTHS WHEN YOU CAN'T)

You see how difficult it becomes when
one tries to get very close to the facts.

RAINER MARIA RILKE *Letters on Cezanne*

Well
could I go
on one wing

DENISE LEVERTOV
"The Wings"

If you watch closely, you will see that water
appears and disappears in the poem.

JACK SPICER *Homage to Creeley*

Explanatory Notes

What we call poetry is the boat.

ROBERT DUNCAN
"A New Poem" (for Jack Spicer)

Come on, Mama
Come with your daughter
To the ragged shadow
It'll be fun

We can be tranquil
By the moon-field

You can say a spell
To calm yourself:

Blossom knit
& heel affix
Fiddle fern
In the neck of the sun

A band of women
stepped over the wall
at the Capitol:

one jumped "gingerly"
toward the police;—

you make an effort
like a moonbeam
washing its body
in the silk of morning

between the x of
window's paradox
& the sea beyond

Light, light
chilly math—

to keep a bold
    interior
reserve of joy

& poetry's record
of symbolic acts—

voice-disk,
risk of meaning

& in the heart
    of the eye, i
felt a hollow hold—

Silence within silence
within silence within—

No cats or dogs
    or geese

No creatures on earth
    when moon spirits ride

Just a family
    playing upstairs

Just the scrape
    of the bone people
inside

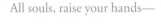

Length passed;
dimension fled;—

(ivy moon
a pale slug eating
a downed poppy)

i had knocked
on the door
   & wept—

& the moon didn't answer
but the door
   with three
corners did—

All souls, raise your hands—

(easier done than said)

i have a little headache,
you said to the word—

& the word described
as water came
in the style of a stem
by a stream
by a stone;

it is wild that you lived,
said the word—

Oak moon, reed moon—

our friend called;
she was telling the pain
what to think.

I said Look. If you
relax you'll get better.

Better? who wants better,
said a moonbeam
under the wire,

the soul is light's
hypotenuse; the lily's
logic is frozen fire—

Suppose you are the secret
of the shore—a strong wave
lying on its side—

you'd come to earth again

(as if joy's understudy
would appear) & you
could live one more bold

day without meaning to,
afresh, on winter's piney floor;

you say, I've been
to the door & wept;
it says, what door

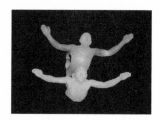

It's twins, you silly—
this irrational eagerness
to be alive:
Romulus & Remus
under a wolf moon—

At sea, whales pass;

in town, *thwack* of politics
on pavement. Soon, sparrows
will come from their districts,

& that one dreadless

thrush: watermarks
on an obelisk—

Jerry-rigged the soul,
which sailed awhile—

heard a world call
Help the little live long
Help the little
live long Help—

Looked over in a
tentative hour,

feeling strong when asked;

& beauty spun around
(somewhat around)
pink as a pronoun

FEBRUARY DAWN   FEBRUARY MOON

The near woke   Over pink eucalyptus
to a not-near   leaves after the eclipse

& in the heart's brief Vermont   the moon's particular
a fricative thaw—   area of having been
                                  shaved looked just like
(The spirits were being   your sore throat—!
extra quiet
so fear could finish   The ancestors looked
its satin chasm);   on, expecting
                                  nothing but the real;
out the window:
ice-insects in a sequence   *what more can we offer,*
                                  they asked you,
& children starting for the woods their ideal—
without their violins—

There was a golden
life before your birth
then love shone
in a flask of dawn:

*can you put them both
in the same place?
Why don't you try.*

So i sat right next to
the tree (advance advance)

& the little wren
came over to me
(advance advance)

Ash moon, seed
moon, green
room, mind:

here's how the first
song goes in time—:

it goes again
it goes again
again—

Don't ask
who I am. I was
the dawn song;
i helped you hide—

When i can't sleep
i count backward
from 10,000

Numbers keep
the letters out
Yes numbers keep
the phrases out

(though sometimes
awake in the braised
fog i think the names

of slightly missing
ones at dawn)

The non-you enters
the you, & morning

also has a dusk,
a texture behind
the hermit thrush,

italic ampersands
in the brush,
&&& &

a form of now
alright all right
a form of then
so bright so bright

MAY MOON

A calm has split your panic,
the halves fall away;

over spikes of grass
& vinegar shadows,
the moon, mildly hopeful
like a little Thursday.

The once-humiliating
gleam has gone;

it expected too much
from the tired faces.
Now the crafty calm can work
not as thing, as a vowel
that might continue—

MAY MOON

Officer, i was speeding
because light sped
like crushed bits of God

seeking more energy

i understand the horse
who broke her front
legs trying to run
i understand that horse

all women understand her
we all understand that
horse we all understand

her all of us do

Light said   *If the tablets*
are written with silence
what good is a prophecy

Light said   *Let's be*
like the mirror we found
in the leaf why don't we

or, that's what
summer said it said

when we made time
past twenty azure frogs
in the pond—or, when
we held time's arrows

Have you lost your
way with technique?

(Try pitching between
other styles
why don't you.)

Night is young but doesn't
lack experience; your hope
flies over the field:
little voice, little fact,

bracelet of signs
for the unknown—

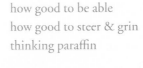

JULY MOON

glamorous game
the gasp
the pillar

i hear your instructions
off to the side

i thought I
knew then new
seeped out

color of citronella

to the cicada
we're a chessboard
in each eye

how good to be able
how good to steer & grin
thinking paraffin

& in that sentence shack
an ache of novelty

my lost watch breathes
in finity
(its minutes were pets!)
its time flocks

& in thy sight
& in thy blister
sight a paradox

AUGUST MOON

A bridesmaid
smile sliced heaven,

a shyness
held inside
the harpist's clause;

the groom stood
indented
in his neon cavern;

& hesitant before
eternity,
joy stood
under the arch—

SEPTEMBER MOON

—ooops! gosh. Trying
to stop being paranoid
about e-mail surveillance—

Barley moon before
the wedding looks like
Mrs. Noah's lifeboat:
one more ride;

you who are here,
you who survive,

apache tomorrow,
throw down the braided rope;
be by my side—

FOUR

(OF LOCAL CREEKS & AQUEDUCTS)

DRAINSHED MAP WATERS
CHANNELED UNDERGROUND
STREAMLIFE SUBTRACTED

NOTICE ON A DRAIN COVER
Santa Monica, California

Water is the limiting factor of everything.

JIMMYE HILLMAN Lecture at Richton
Mississippi Rotary Club, c. 1953

Its house is the letter Bet

EUGENE OSTASHEVSKY
"Third Water Poem"

Temporary tattoos contain permanent dyes.
Please look over your room to be certain there are
no stains so you will not be charged for the damage.

MARINA PACIFIC MOTEL Venice, California

Baffled dread one day,
hope the next; hope
shifts; dread returns, then
that also lifts. Sometimes
in California, hearing sentences
like, "The storm gates
have opened," or "Storms
have lined up out
into the Pacific," you
experience a cheerful scraping
between depression & what's
here; in Portuguese, *saudades*—
there's no English equivalent.
Crows over coast live
oaks, laurel saplings covered
with lichen veils in
oat-grass fields. The moon
is in *Gort*, Celts
might say. Ivy dies,
clinging. You drive along
thinking of a friend
who has forgiven you;
vineyards very gold, that
gold of school pencils.

The waters flow over the people of California
They flow over bodies in distressed desire
Pocks & knots & fixed muscles
With names hooked to their types
Women who left snacks in white boxes
With metal handles in fuel-efficient cars
Where the first oak on the right side turns down
Tatter peril stressform fear
West of where serpentine peeks ragged from the years
West of vertical ice paradox parhelia
& pines smelling of vanilla
Where they lay in their mineral calm

We asked the glitter in the vineyard
You still there?
Tatter peril stressform matter
Under the vineyard how shall we live
With nouns for seasons & chthonic patter
Where everything happens as itself

Steam rose from the geyser it rose & fell
Into vernal pools from vertical ice
Ragged from the years
Rose with a mildly worried look on its face
With specks of rivers & nouns can't you tell
From being so long in the seasons so well
Steam from the geyser it rose & fell
With dried-up crying from the sea can't you tell
& the flavor of the dream
Was the flavor of death
You can probably hear it as the crow's wing *crrr crr*
Where the pine on the right side dips down

Ash ash we lower ourselves into you
With the help of little Eve
We lower our hearts & our chromosomes
& ex-wives & Spanish clouds
Sisters & brothers of the unkilled dream
Where we lay in our mineral calm

Stressform fear carbon & tatter
Minerals pushed up from the sea floor so well
Calcium boron sulfur
Fluoride silicates & salts
Do you hate your body did you ever oh hell
You need to stop that right now said water
It flowed over bodies with tattoos
Of prime time & bridges
Tendrils of grapes & lilies & Spanish clouds
Tattoos of lovers' names & flexible worlds
It flowed over each woman disordered in the west
Where the fern on the left side drips down

You searched for water but you were one of it o well
Minor streams said goodbye they rose & fell
The y of water like wishbones & still
A fluke a creek sound breaks through up north
Till the body of a woman is the body of a world
Where you live in your mineral calm

You have arrived with great effort
You lived at the edge of the field like a wasp gall
With knots & pocks & fixed muscles by the well
With burls & girls & Spanish clouds
So if death had visited you what would it have said
Where the vine on the hillside winds down
Days of dried-up crying by split-apart oaks

Sea joined by your son for a season
& if life had visited you
What would it have said
Peril stressform carbon joy
Where you slept for a time beyond reason

LOCAL WATER & THE UNIVERSAL SEA

A molecule steps perpetually

               into the present.

      It will let go to blend;

it rotates a power

                   to western willow groves

        from marshes or ice quilts quite east,

that not one new drop shall be slighted

      till it is dew,

           till government hopes blue

          into the longing system   of the molecule;

it haunts & is haunted,

       brooding & laughing in western yellow groves.

               Look out, Senator—!

           perilous little word couplings—

(after George Herbert)

From hills, from storm drains
meeting tumbled-below molecules of Berkeley
tap water & rain, past Center & Shattuck to the cool straight
waves of the Bay, Council, daylight that Creek. Near CementHenge
of the B of A with the Shattuck Cinemas' mild butter Saturday matinee
popcorn redolence meets downtown Peets' decaf, daylight. Daylight pos-
sible lizards, raccoons, beetles which starts with be, their esplanade & vis-
ion. Corridors would return for vision citizens, also dew on finches flying
to Dwight. Council, apply your   wisdom. We swear by the seven
creeks of Berkeley, as by our   poetry—for e.g. A's, AW's, B's, B
H's, Bateau Group's, XX's C's, CS's, D's, D's, E's, F's, FH's, G's, G's, GG's
& GO's, XX's & I's, J's, JB's & JC's, JF's, JJ's, JM's, K's & KS's, L's, LH's,
LM's, LS's, M's, MP's, N's, P's, XX's & PD's, PS's, R's, RS's, RP's who
moved, S's, SK's, T's, U-Z's, XX's, XX's, all students living over win-
dows who walk near spearmint nooses of campus creeksides,
who write little or much, in water as in poetry— that we
are one body. (Shelley noted this.) The invisible
is lined with the visible.
(We also noted this.) Aren't you mostly water
yourselves? We walked to campus on Watershed Day against
our national government. Water creatures are against war. Even
the swordfish nearby knows not to send its sword into another sword-
fish unless it's going to eat it. So water leaped to brown. The soul of the
poet, healing, saw the leaping. Be on the side of leaping, Council. Aren't
the first two letters of Be   rkeley legally curved? So the dryads
living near this Creek leave   oaky ghost menus, words of ances-
tors CM, JM, JS, TG & letters from the east, from A-Z, C & F who
should have moved here, N& J, J & B who did move— So the visible
improves in a School where they said daylight the creek, day-light.
& the Aging sheen caught the Bay. We don't know how to live
but water thinks it through, a syntax tangled to renew, $H_2O =$
one-third forever & two-thirds good sense. Spirals & hips,
eyelashed willows, we're yours; what else lives? In
water, we stop stopping it—

There's so much about the mind
we don't know yet between the mem-
orable & the forgotten which is why
we need water words. The clogged-for-50-
years-creek tumbled along badly when the
father & brother of the brenda who transcribes
this worked on campus; when the first husband
worked here, the creek was dirty— just a dump—
& in the era of the second husband, clearing began.
They tried bunchgrass & a Study formed. Live oaks drop-
ped their spiky leaves on down, Council, & the creek had a
chance, its numbers & properties like mythic figures— Daphne
& her agitators— in M's word, to *toggle* back & forth between new
things they said. Wholeness lives in parts like those water striders,
triremes of golden insects, Council. (It's up to you to make brave gov-
ernment imagine things.) Sacramento suckers had returned, hitch-
minnow, the raccoon who fished them out; & the egret that fished
was probably even helping the salmon. Maybe you'll put porous
pavers for the Berkenstocks, my dears. This great stream
of Strawberry Creek, with its stickle-backs like the
letter E at the end of Mother Tuolumne carry-
ing the muskrat from Cascadia's borderland,
is three point five miles long, Council. We are
not on the side of extra starts but of inner free-
dom. Let's note to each lover of rain-checks that
economy & strains of longing come from the same
place. Feed creatures. Dolphins near Monterey dive,
Council, when the creek's mysterious ochre balances
in health. Fine mist is curling in the brenda hairs.
The lyric grew in strength & the water grew less dead.
Some have a moment of mood when they stand on the bridge
near the U.C. Life Sciences Building. The cottonwood says twenty-
five things & a lamp. Monarchs will come back from Reno & Win-
nemuca; buckeye, father of the camphor tree, would talk. Nymphs
would make do with celebrate. Sisters & brothers of the Council,
bring light, beauty & order to the edge; we the writers & readers,
griots with lyres & harps, in you, by you & for the generations,
ask that you day light that creek day, day ∘ light ∘ that ∘ Creek

The farmers' market is breaking down;
fringed sagging canopies fold inward
like the Renaissance. Wrestlers & jugglers
enter the park; slightly soggy boxes
are being flattened as pineapple guavas
finally relax & a chill comes over
the waist of autumn. From Happy
Boy Organic Farms come bottles of
thick-as-infinity apple juice with its
ankles of pulp. Early tangelos, late
plums, Shinko pears cut into tender
celadon wedges, mute mache. Women in
oversized aprons wash knives in Berkeley
tap. Tap. Berkeley tap-tap. The runoff
joins culverts of the creek &
hurries to the Bay. Mists of
elemental sense hover over crates of
fruit as hybrids cohabitate. Men too
smart to pray talk with men
too smart not to. Terraces of
almonds, piles of ridged hazelnuts &
tubs of hot dal. Marjoram, stalks
of lavender & limp dill. Chips
for sampling tomatillo salsas. You have
entered the market with your beloved,
your souls like drops of water
easily merged. Water tumbles from
the east, trickles under the huge
blond radishes, dark parsley, big broccoli
rabe & mustard greens, beneath only
slightly popular bitter melons, baskets of
trench-coat gray sunflower seeds, flat &

curly kale, unruly rainbow chard, under
raisiny balsamic vinegar from Sonoma &
tables of Big Paw Olive Oil,
violet grapes, girls with yo-yos, boys
doing Tai Chi, beneath smart, worried-
looking Berkeley babies slumped in very
expensive strollers while their mothers eat
carob-coated pretzels & their fathers eat
floppy artichoke pizza slices. The inside
of a dream is itself; the world
is ways to have considered it.
Down goes Berkeley water under jars
of twice-born tan-oak & Sierra wildflower
honey, trays of porcini mushrooms, calm
shitakis & gold parasol chanterelles from
secret locales. Everything that happens is
so odd; it enters matter over
& over as mystical names. Blue
Heron Farms. Phonemes in water join
sixteen kinds of Napa tomatoes all
glitter & rondure next to nets
of persimmons—the big kind that
will ripen, the squat kind that
can't. Wings of purple & green
cabbages the size of musicians' heads
open next to squashes with spiders
pretending to be speckles. Sexy peaceful
spinaches will be new next week
as will the fennel smelling of
licorice, lyric Fujis from Blossom Bluff
Orchards round as depictions of time
in dreams, globes of baby eggplants,
pods of cardamom, planets of pocked
oranges, chestnuts, & radical fabric hearts
of pomegranates covered by motiveless fog—

THE COVENANT

Having stopped using dolphins to locate explosives in the Cold War
they had 30 leftover dolphins.

An officer noted that to move them to open waters would endanger them.

One dolphin taking part in all this smiles like a Boy Scout counting knives—

(how do they smell explosives under the sea)

(who had once taken souls to the beyond)

Before the second marriage i greeted middle age;
should i wear reading glasses at the wedding?

(& : how to keep up w/ the spirit world— whose figures
          seemed distant, cool—)

These bodies we'll know only a few more decades
    have become a series of yeses;   yes to capillaries & leg veins' h's,
          to x's on hands bathed in aloe & sweet peppermint,

yes to face lines so western—

When the officer shows concern by squinting,
one especially tame dolphin puts its nose— what looks like a child's knee—
          into the officer's hand.

EARTH'S SHADOW

(Squaw Valley Meadow)

My marmot hath early come

to the field

from its twin caves inasmuch as i

could see the action of its sleeker

fur, after its nap of being seen

by the mycorrhizal web below

(like Hildegaard visiting her tent of eyes—)

on the granite mountain that floats on its

shadow

& i say i adjure thee

by the deer & the open sleeves of the olive-sided flycatcher,

say, how far did you go? For we want to know

the qualities we cannot know—

By empathic pine that leans

which way & that,

emerges by yarrow

in one more solar-eating summer,

by the black ant & thy quite hopping flea, from the

heptane-holding Jeffrey pine puzzle bark,

& by Clark's nutcrackers' seed-storing frenzy with its tongue stored in back of its

eyes, say what earth does below.

What makes the mountain rise

while its shadow pulls it

down instead? Maybe the very

ice age relic roots under the 7-11 & the new ski supply place

grow

from this

change, above which mice harvest shell points of the

tangled

persia tridenata. (Now you my civilian run over & beg like the letter E)—

When i think of our human shame, how the handwriting

cloud shunneth us, how the human shadow

is unknown to us,   how though we seek help from

scrub oak with gall-fortress wasp pupae then

mouthless adults emerge,

& yet you marmot run

above earth's shadow between us & soil not imploring but for one sunflower

snack or a piece of my veggie wrap,

can you say if below

the many sounds there is a single sound. Scratch

thy left ear for Yes & thy right for No. & though

we have done thy

habits disservice by feeding thee much junk,

yet the air plankton & swallow might restore when we are gone & our

kind, gone—

A fat robin has come out like patience with rufous feathers

seeking light shards & the sprinklers start, too puffed

for normal use. Thou marmot. How was thy nap.
In thy cave like Hildegaard

sleeping upside down in *ERUTAN*
                         NATURE
you could
read the earth. As the five of blacks in the bluejay crest disappeared to the
opposite rill,
        hops the high canopy
over the can't-stand-the-tractors purr, tell us
what is the shadow of earth,
i adjure thee by every beetle
    burrowing the overwhelm to xylum & avena ring;
        & though my shame is great
        & i cannot make up our minds about anything
                    o my civilian,
thou might abide a moment here in this tissue syntax,
                marmot with the sleek silver who hath traveled long within
                        the earth & seen others angle the snow come winter,
        who hath not seen the web be not more than one everything
with life trance & decay, tarry while
we think on thee, stay—

My anarchist talks while i'm driving
    (i'm tired but she is thriving—)
       beside pylons in flood plains, near
          marshes, culverts & storm drains, in
             amethyst mornings & clear, past exiled
             gulls, veils of oil, sooty dancers
               & streams that are sometimes enough.
           We must do something but what,
        she asks. Pheasants fly into ditches;
      fields bubble & broaden. The unknown
     Future waits wrapped in itself like
a larva, almost alive & awake—

HYDROLOGY OF CALIFORNIA

AN ECOPOETICAL ALPHABET

There's a river   of rivers   in California   beyond   all earthquakes
bringing   coiled water   from the north It is grammar when we are anxious
in our days   bringing tumble   from freshets   north of Klamath   where
redwoods release fog drops
ceaselessly from filtered tops   Steelhead   Coho   salmon the few that do
to Humboldt   past dams   hereafter   known as   /   where streams/ like
colorless   green ideas leap furiously/ where the Eel River flooding 753,000
feet per second /sees
fewer eels than before
Future of poetry   there's a stream *between a & b* as i write this   a dream
of a west   that would outlast us/   if we were life   which we are   drops
from Trinity ice storms   to Smith River & down   North Coast regions
brighter   seaside towns with
two waitresses named Pam
Future of poetry   i saw a black-faced gull   a juvenile   awaiting neap tide
We use the word *neap*   to mean   purple runnels/   Banks gathered wild force
at the edge of names Mattole Navarro /Hearts gathered wild force electrons
trading energy for food
Future of poetry Let's move   between emotions in hydropoetics for i   am a
pilgrim with no progress recalling rivers   when we were anxious
past   wetlands needing every turning time/ more than people   need
little dams for arugula
Many had lawns   They had to shower/ They had to eat   i said to main brenda
Now don't start   just ignorantly criticizing state   dams   the whole time
You drink gallons of it you know you do / We followed creeks through decades
left of where eagles
can eat whole deer
Stopped·   near Fort Ross   We looked up to redwoods   releasing beads fog
drops   The women so kind in Mendocino   They took the beyond   & ran
with it You wrote on the memory tablets/ Blind sticks arranged themselves

Water-bearer was your star
Our settlements   didn't last
nor should they have   nor should they   There were economics & lifestyles
after   explorers made possible the cogs/ .00001 percent in rain fell
down /We stood & loved   south/ of the delicate eerie lighthouse at
Point Arena   where griefless
the sea lions loll

There's a quiver of rivers   the Sacramento   We saw a pleasant pheasant
near a pylon in the Delta   its back a walking rainbow   in 100,000 acres
they saved the *they*   who can save\ We don't hate developers or do we
We hate their greed
those butt-ugly buildings   Actually
butts are adorable compared to Gated communities/ the poor buildings
can't even cry   though wild radish loves them   *Raphanus raphanistrum*
"common in disturbed places" Maltese crosses each flower a shadow/
violet   in its means/
We ran near why-worry
levees & one time one of the developers said Well you wouldn't want
to live in a tee-pee now would you brenda   Future of poetry   we saw
dactylic glomerata   Leaves of grasses\ i don't honestly mind the word
introduced   as in introduced species *between c & d* dogtail grasses *cynosurus*
echinatus Near the Capitol
assemblymembers were drinking Fanta
near a fanning floodplain/ coots with white beaks east of Feather River
between e & f trace horse gold rush \boys picking pyrite from the North
Fork & 2 waitresses named Toni   Gold must be so glad in heaven
glad & gold are

brothers w/ different mothers
The lovely   & a bit dammed American River\ mergansers & brome/
buffleheads like reverse Oreos   rice fields\ algae from phosphates Such
afternoons   might seem owned O unrushed dream of time i saw some
earthly flapping in the
rushes/ swallows eating pounds
of gnats/ & both shall row My love & i leaned   on our tailbone The
Giants were ahead   for a change in someone's earphones A fundraiser for
fucked-up rivers History turned half our faces golden for a change\A
day so bright
we could not hear
the paradox set up by Being   Then Gary yelled Hey   & a tall cloud
passed by like a yoga teacher   Inside each seed\   didn't look like
competition but floated forever from us to you Future of poetry
We wanted not   to fear human life   to know as molecules know like
water from a book

There's a shiver   of rivers north of Shasta that melts   when we are faster
storms split   the plus signs   lava   flowed from night caves   marshes
with magpies   that dipped like punk nuns   we kept the word "beauty"
in mind for Shastina
that upside-down bride 75%
of H_2O slides   from north of Tahoe\ 1685 feet deep *high into nothingness*
Twain wrote   where some say   the dead sink frozen in their costumes
Future of poetry we entered   the howling edges of a dream   looked back to
Celestial City   texted each
other & soon whole
words will be gone   c u l8r   will remain But rain loves the day like haiku
River goes out   river comes in like a cat\ googled *eutrophication* for June so

that   no word should die New words shall sprout   in dreams beyond time
Trout spawned *chasmistes cujus/*
We saw some types
of knotting   in nature *between g & h*   What should we call those silvery
gray parenthesis-type things   hanging off   lodge pole pines Don't colonize
that tree by naming it   a nameless poet said   Lucky he doesn't have to
hunt for his food
a naming poet said
The pine at the end   of the mind   Life from Life   Form from Form Be-
gotten not sprayed   Of one being with the Mother   Through Her rough
cones were made   \We hiked Desolation noted streaky granites moraines
condensation   infiltration evaporation chanted
Byzantium past Shirley Lake
You pronounced it *Byzanseeum*   needleminer moths *what peeves you* David
said a fly-catcher said perched in blister rust   bitterbrush needing mouse-
shit for its   pilgrim's process/   under fluttering twisted braids   cirrus clouds
Leaves of grasses' panicles
reduced in mountain air
slowed down *between i & j*   ice age relic trees *populus tremuloides*
we worried less   Glaciers beneath Boreal & Tui chub melts down to Walker
Lake   *pelecanus erythrorhynchos* if not too salty for them   if not but extinction
lasts forever in its
rivers from a book

There's a sliver   of rivers   west of Napa which rhymes   when we are happy
its timed relation   to high heat   makes cuneiform of grapevines   snappy
sharpshooters' wings are glassy   hills blonde as conference coffee/   tawny

paws of mountain lions
trout declined   Lake Berryessa
our hope for the good\ Dragonflies with six ankles   over lightest summer
Entered a cool winery   saw oaken caskets   in earth's wild force   You pushed
on in your shivers   don't make pilgrim's progress /please   greet us forever
between k & l
sages & mugwort where
nostalgia happens forward / County Fair not Vanity   Sweet girls in black
hoodies   alienated labor & Karmel Korn a cloying   smell tho'   Karmel
Korn is also nature   Future of Poetry an oak spoke to me as i walked
on the mountain not
like God speaking to
Bush about Iraq   The creek was full of trash & origins/ It said search *between*
m & n for what we have destroyed   & both shall row on Papermill Creek   my
love & i   saw huge   orange nonsense dragonflies like fire engines medium
bluets   like tiny folded
pool cues & green
ones of unimaginable luster On winter Fridays paper snowflakes taped
on Inverness School windows   County funding drying up so only one
snowflake per child   Seeds of herbs dreaming in their packets at Toby's
Future of poetry Everything
feels everything i don't
just think so   i know so Lagunitas Creek feels ridged horsetails push up
from the Precambrian   Beetles fringed gourds fleabane   under July sky   feels
big old see-through ferns   red currents There are half-emotions between all
officially recognized emotions i
said to the lady
in buckeyes' sacred grove *syncaris pacifica* sulfur butterflies California sisters
cabbage whites west coast ladies   western tiger swallowtail riparian rhymes
with carrion   cowbird w/ the oil-spill neck   walks   like a hieroglyph\
at Coast Camp near
wood-rats' nests like
water from a book

There's a giver   of rivers   the Central coast   & you would go   almost
if you   were a you instead of a Future   which you are   w/ all the santas
Santa Inez   Santa Cruz   An owl waits nearby   *cathartes aura* 14 bones
in its head   directional
hearing   owls aren't really
wise   they turn south to hear   poor kids' guns going off   at Travis Airforce
orders are given   between fogdrops/   money flies &   money wrongs
the Pacific   This pilgrim   makes no progress   in her flight   a marbled
murrelet feeding at sea
nesting in old-growth redwood
Future of poetry i
saw shorebirds   choking on shy crabs   shaking sand off   bull kelp   tossed
from the deep   Gulls look like girls   quickly judging   each other's purses
Now Democrats also say offshore drilling   isn't too bad/ You came to me
in a dream beyond
time\This life you
sang   in   your off-key way   *between o & p*   old moon-laden & tawdry   we drove
near Salinas a river Steinbeck called "part-time"   fields of garlic   red-legged
frogs in flood plains   Sang to me quite tenderly   *between q & r*   Carmel   had
steelhead once   & pond
turtles their   necks ridged
like destiny   The stream flowed right past Tor House   steelhead your   *onchor-*
hyncus mykiss   funny that trout has *mykiss* in its name   Yes i know i know
humans can't not play golf   Geese pull worms through agricultural   runoff
pooling on side lawns
Does use feel bad
i asked the worms   being pulled   Silver butterflies   feeding   on deer shit
parasite *anthopleura elegantissima*   My love & i so busily drove   to a poetry
reading past   fuzzy artichokes   near Gilroy   Prophet thistles w/streams
that drop   near Santa Cruz
How shall we live
& they indicated   as if John Muir replied   *so low a human voice cannot hear*
you   want   your tomatoes   don't you   You want Almond Delite   & golf
You want   to drink Sprite   w/runnels   of gravy   at Denny's\faces in

laminated menus windsurfing widows This is the price   the stream went

refugees in aqueducts like

water from a book

The deliver of rivers   the San Joaquin   that blends when we are minor

with broken strings & finer in port towns near Carquinez saline marinas

south Delta bevels   near 57 levees the age main brenda is now writing this

The soul is the

water & the aqueduct

transferred to the slough at some point   i love the word *slough*   Could

write it all day long   Slew of sloughs down off 99 Saw rough-cut Berenda

Slough   pumping H_2O costs more than it makes\ under Hetch-Hetchy

they named after seeds

2.1 million acre feet

into   the Aqueduct past Merced   Papery onion skins flying off trucks   A

billboard signed by Jesus   Desire saved   the Chinook 130,000 & now only

100   in Tuolumne\ 2 waitresses named Debbie   bad snowpack year so

almost no veil at

Bridalveil Falls but delicate

mists   tumbled & a

Clark's nutcracker flew thru them   Future of Poetry *between* s *&* t   We saw

a meadow spirit   a high vortex in the years of writing this hydro-ecopoetics

Snow sparkles/ Thou shalt flow down after dusk Vernal Falls downvalley

Cusumnes/ Fields of sticky

tarweed   pressed ham   in

convenience stores & the H_2O tastes   a little chemically in Fresno We

miss   Larry Levis   crystal music of his forms/   Future of Poetry This is
your Watershed said Pam   We saw rain enter a saint's mouth Interviewed
an irrigation ditch Pray
for us San Joaquin
alleged granddaddy of Jesus   Pray backward like a feeling   Pray for river
Merced Pray JS keeps some world in a poem   so fertilizer won't kill him
Headwaters hitched to Slurpees 7-11 swimming pools in Stockton Saw
chlorine clouds of infinity
we drank from Pardee
Reservoir Sweated w/ enchantment 90 miles away   Hitched others in the
watery beyond/ Hitched to the others we drank/   If you think you're alone
You haven't learned the language   i gave you snow ^^^ from sugar pines
falls to you in
water for your book

The   forgiver of rivers near Tulare   that flowed when we were sorry
His vocabulary didn't do it all/ Drinking did a little A central
California basin\ that couldn't find the ocean   Why do you write like this
a man asked me
Because sir i am
a sorceress looking for my sources   Because sir we were diverted/ like a
river to mid-heaven by early salt & late capitalism We had a progress spasm/
snowdrops to Kern chasm 13,000 feet   Does use feel bad i asked my love
as dark cast its
opening   *salma aquabonita* &
groundwater spun below   desiring to tender us perfectly unexampled 6.5 acre
feet per year to an aquifer It did not flow from the grief tent Tule

River   Skunks & badgers   willow flycatcher *epidonax traillii*   we
want to see u
between u & v
yellow-billed cuckoo/ Agribusiness did it to our vocabulary   Preoccupied
the joy w/spray   & amber waves   of gray A woman stands   over her sage-
brush with a hose   in the heat   we drive through Bakersfield   & one time
at a truck stop
i observed the flavored
condoms on a twirling rack could hardly wait to tell Mary   *i'm not fucking*
kidding u   hot-fudge coconut cream pie condoms & piña colada ones also
/We read in the guidebook   elegy words *once formed* as in "once formed
Tulare Lake" That made
me mad as Jeffers
What about one itty-bitty bomb on a dam *pow- * Use asterisks instead
No ecoterror for the coyote   it had a hurt foot   for even rats are scarce
Designated Wilderness   go river-rafting/ They're shooting deer   not for
food   We carry the burden not the act   i did not break our noun yet i did
drink from that well
i drank to the
end of time   Took way too many showers for my *lifestyle* that's my least
favorite word   4500 gallons per day   Went we we wee all the way
to Tehachipi/   & amber waves of avena   & *i who had seen was implicated* all
the way home like
crying from a book

There's   a trickle of rivers   the South Lahontan   that exits from
a fountain Mono Lake's three-salt condition   chlorate sulfate   &
carbons Trout came back thank god When this poet says   god she
means god of   particular

daughters/   Owens north fork

River   god of bitter waters / god of half- existence   desert god so
so erotic you know you're loved   already by god of tumbleweed god
of truck-stop coffee   god of better get over it   get over Sarah Palin
In the Quaternary Period
when i was almost
living   i prayed to Mary Austin   crinkly places in her spirit Mulholland
stole   her water/ L.A. poets knew it   power rhymes w/shower
poor Mojave River & Earth will know the source   When this poet says
god she means god
of pupfish god of
Joseph Reddeford Walker survivor in the spine/   Some folks   think malls
in deserts are nice grasses pretending to be native   brine shrimp will return
/flies of alkali *Ephydra hians* lowest meets the highest   Mt. Whitney &
Death Valley *soul* &
soil exact same word
except for u & i
Future of poetry i saw the great heart in a mirror /Land grew around it
but i have not seen the Amargosa vole found there   i have not seen *vireo*
belli pusillus i saw inland seas   Osiris fetched from hydrogeologic edges
from Barstow balmy Palmdale
an Affordable Housing Aqueduct
It *does not serve water to the region*/Put on Sleater-Kinney to drive there   but
never quite arrived there diverted in 1940 like a good lie think Faye Dun-
away in *Chinatown* don't abandon what you hope for   when you brush my
teeth in Hesperia please
turn the faucet off
Visit us now o vole *before the w & x*   visit us now *rhinichthys osculus*   visit us
now alluvial   alluvial bearded spangletop   bees in their boxes & we who
had lived were implicated between slopes We climbed the dome & went
home w/a history of
glaciers in a book

There's a river of nevers   the South Coast   where some would like it
most   if there   were a river   which there were   by gum by the fall of
capitalism   The banks crash as we write this We had a pilgrim's regress
crazy brenda & her
sorceress She ran with
her love on the boardwalk   The marine layer grows fatter/ over 13
million travelers   You know that part in *Vertigo* when Kim Novak jumps
backward in the Bay   *It looks like a set* he said *but it was filmed on location*
That part   on the
other hand   he said
holding her other hand   *was filmed in a tank in Los Angeles* We are about
out of time   O three-spine stickleback O word riparian   O valley oak
over Santa Monica   o black walnut plowed under long ago   Visit us now
in our   maritime routes   Visit us now *Tetradymia spinosa*   cotton-thorn
Visit us now in
the hour of our
need Visit us now in the hour of our seed   of cord grass & Gray's fescue
Visit us now in the hour   over San Gabriel short-awn foxtail & fluff grass
bent grass & blue grama   Visit us now in the hour of our native & non-
tree that made Hollywood
Dear love i'm tired
Let's go to bed Maybe a college girl is reading this when we're a little
dead O girl please mind your watershed   Take care of crazy poets
Visit the inner-net   In the end   there will be a rupture
said Walter whose arcade
thought up the Web
We are freckles of sun   We are sleeping in the poem   Shoppers stand
in the little shops   They don't know what to buy We lie at the Shangri La
between z & y No one knows   how this sentence will end in a dream
with a lyric   sky
Visit us Joni Mitchell
Visit us   Future of Poetry with a solitude of streamlets into a local
pond the mind at the end of the palm   Nothing was gone when we
saw that bird   We saw its feathers as water It was in & out of time

NEAP TIDE

We showed our life a spring of steel

Here is some knowledge
brought with a merciless cry

It was a season of feasts & vents
past the season of suicides

Night after night the same
complaint like an ignorant wave
tossing itself in helpless repetition

Dawn after dawn headlights across water
melting with stars in purple runnels of the bay

The knowledge of unreachable signs

of intervals uncrossable even in dreams

of meaning transforming itself like a bride

saw changing into *was*
tide the backward edit of a tide

Take it back we cried
pouring a cup of staggering
for the beautiful seer of this life

as in a play when
libations are offered to earth
though that was never a requirement really

& knowledge went back to the purple sea
& merciful love stood by our side

STILL POINTS IN WATER

The lookful page
is watching with its seeds
of extra time; as a mother
      sowed the cosmos, so the page—

as a shadow sews a pocket.

Plant your feet to the rogue
whistle of the sun
      near interim flowers, waxy
      Cactus & little Friendly.

Demeter sowed the thrice-furrowed
      field with feathers from the ditch—

You make your expressions; psalms
visit you; pinnate roses
      wheel the fall, pinched by
      summer lightning storms.

You write by the window:
dust from a bronze age
      loved by day. You are present.

You are here in what you said & say,
      each vowel a cave
      with two doors—

(for my mother)

1 /

You traveled, your mind set forward
slightly like your father's watch.
You went toward the blurred edges
to make a skin of now, of later.
The place of origins included
dust that spoke, the particle spirits,
a hawk with its droplet of blood,
an armored toad.
Ancestors looked on. You etched
letters with a stick, making matter
of the beautiful & the felt.

3 /

Your loved ones gather strength
after an illness; they put their heads
against the years. They hear
the molecular rattle of the mesquite,
the finding bin of syllables,
their mothers' unchanging breath.
They ask what is possible, given
the wretched governments of earth.
A poem can't do much but
it gives off sparks from its wheels,
the bristle & the clicks, mostly
at moments of resistance.

2 / *(a divination)*

The first symmetry was lawless.
You had to invent water,
to pull meaning from form—
a darkness between rhythms—
& always at the edge of noon
in pale pavilions & ramadas of straw,
your practice coded in shadow,
the sweet promise of a visitor's well.
Remember the dream of a little owl?
It came willingly to your hands, &
everything quivered around
where it flew in—

4 /

—& when you went out in the world
after the long disease of yourself
& saw the colors of the world
right before they arrive, the dulls
& browns of the absolute season,
mauves streaming in the waters
of a year, you knew the features
of the world are the same
as the language of the soul
& by traveling in those elements
you'd lose your fear—

ACKNOWLEDGMENTS & NOTES

—Thanks to editors & staff of periodicals & other venues in which this work has appeared or is forthcoming: alhambrapublishing.com, *American Poet, At Length, Back Room Live (Life Long Press), Berkeley Poetry Review, Best American Poetry 2008, Bombay Gin, Bright Wings: An Anthology of Poems About Birds, Burnside Review, Caffeine Destiny, Colorado Review, Columbia: A Journal of the Arts, Columbia Poetry Review, Conjunctions, The Contra Costa Times, Crate, Critical Quarterly, Drunken Boat, Earth First!, Electronic Poetry Review,* Em Press, Empyrean Press, *Freeverse, From the Sky to the Sea: Poems of the San Francisco Bay Area Watershed, Gulf Coast, Hayden's Ferry Review,* HildaMagazine.org, *The Journal, Lana Turner, Lumina, Lyric Postmodernisms: An Anthology of Innovative Poetries, Meena,* Minuteman Press & Mrs. Dalloway's, *Modern Review, The New Yorker, Northwest Review, Octopus,* Old Crow Press, *Packingtown Review,* Pamirs Poetry, *Ploughshares,* poemsfortheplanet.org, *Poetry Flash, Poetry Northwest,* Poltroon Press, *Pool, Smartish Pace, Sonora Review, Sous Rature, State of the Union: An Anthology of Political Poetry, Superstition Review, Update, Waterstone Review, VanGogh's Ear* (Paris), *Viz Inter-Arts Event: A Trans-genre Anthology, Volt, The Washington Post "Poet's Choice," Wildlife, Women's Work: Modern Women Poets Writing in English.* "To a Desert Poet" was presented to the University of Arizona Poetry Center. Thanks to Andrew Kenower, Quemadura, & Sharon Zetter for help with the manuscript. I am indebted to Frances Lerner & to my family, especially to Bob Hass.

—Notes: "Ballad at the State Capitol" intersperses quotes from Hammurabi's Code of Law, 1750 BCE; CodePink's Working Group for AJR36, especially Sam Joi, facilitated a resolution to bring home the National Guard from Iraq & Afghanistan; it was defeated in the California State Assembly Veterans' Committee when three Democrats didn't show up to vote. "The Eighties" owes a debt to Leonard Michaels's "In the Fifties" & is dedicated to JS. Ashur Etwebi, Helen Hillman, Dora Malech, Yngvil Molaug Haugen, & Eugene Ostashevsky provided names of blackbirds. "Autumn Fugue" is for DY. Part 2 opener: To the woman at the Heritage Foundation who pushed us out: here you are. The reportorial poems derive from Congressional hearings i attended with CodePink 2005–2008. "Near the Great Arch" is for SJB. "Permission to Be Strange" is for HMS. The Heraclitus quote is from Guy Davenport's translation. The moon poems are dedicated to poets & artists, except for "may moon"—for JP (a scholar) and "june moon"—for BZ (a pitcher). "Anthem for Aquifers" is for CDW. "Berkeley Water" is for JV & AW. "Hydrology of California" is dedicated to the Bateau Group & owes debts to the work of David Carle, David Lucas, Jeffrey F. Mount, Standard Schaefer, Chris Sindt, & Gary Snyder as well as to International Rivers, River of Words, & Watershed. "Neap Tide" is for LAM & CL.

Photos are my own digital efforts except as follows: "Reportorial Poetry"—Scooter Libby sentencing by Liz Hourican. "A Violet in the Crucible"—Liz Hourican & police officers by Medea Benjamin. "In a House Committee on Electronic Surveillance"—Boston Tea Party 1846 lithograph in public domain. Part 3: "october moon" —helmet from a display on body armor in the Rayburn Building by Desiree al-Fairooz; Josephine Hass as Pink Vadar by Fiona Hass; "november moon"—Tilden Park newt by Catra Corbett; Desiree al-Fairooz & Condoleezza Rice by Charles Dharapak (Associated Press); "december moon"—lily & Robert Taplin's "Neptune" by Robert Hass; "january moon"—Pt. Reyes lighthouse by Paul Ebenkamp; Ella Hass by Louisa Michaels; "february moon"—amanita mushroom by Hazel Magoon; action at Berkeley Marine Recruiting Station by Janet Weil; "march moon" cactus by Deb Thompson; "april moon"—Audrey Marrs by anonymous; thrush by Jason R. Finley http://www.birdsofwestwood.com/birdpages/hermitthrush.htm; "may moon"— Berkeley owlets by R. L. Sivaprasad, www.birdsofthebay.com; Cornelia Nixon & her horse Sky by Deb Dawson; "july moon"—Squaw Valley meadow by Brett Hall Jones. Part 4: Tilden Park heron by Ethan Michaels. Some images of aqueducts & dams are from Clyde Johnson, the California State Water Project & U.S. Department of Water Resources websites.

ABOUT THE AUTHOR

Brenda Hillman is the author of seven collections of poetry and, with Patricia Dienstfrey, the editor of *The Grand Permission: New Writings on Poetics and Motherhood* (2003). She is the Olivia Filippi Professor of Poetry at Saint Mary's College and works with CodePink, a social justice organization against war.